BRITAIN'S CENTURY
WAR, CONFLICT AND DISSENT

Press Association

BRITAIN'S CENTURY

WAR, CONFLICT AND DISSENT

MAINSTREAM
PUBLISHING

EDINBURGH AND LONDON

First published in Great Britain in 1999 by
MAINSTREAM PUBLISHING COMPANY (EDINBURGH) LTD
7 Albany Street
Edinburgh EH1 3UG

ISBN 1 84018 288 1

A catalogue record for this book is available from the British Library

Designed by Janene Reid
Typeset in Gill Sans Light
Printed and bound in Great Britain by Butler and Tanner Ltd

Suffragette Emmeline Pankhurst in
the polling booth, 1910.

Facing page: Emmeline Pankhurst in a prison dress during a spell in jail.

The siege of January 1910 at 100 Sidney Street, Houndsditch, east London, where troops and police fought a gun battle with three 'anarchists'. The house caught fire and burned to the ground after Home Secretary Winston Churchill refused to allow the fire brigade to intervene. Two bodies were found in the ruins.

Police and troops escorting a convoy past a strike meeting in Liverpool, January 1911.

An incident during the Liverpool railway strike of 1911.

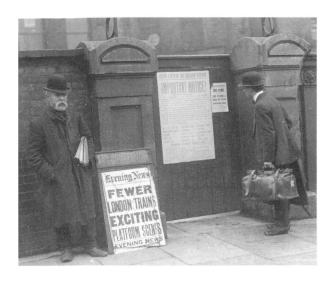

Snow Hill station, London, closed due to a coal strike in 1911.

Protest cut short by the long arm of the law: a suffragette is apprehended by the railings at Buckingham Palace, 1914.

The scene outside the enlisting office in London's Throgmorton Street, after the outbreak of the First World War, August 1914.

A British soldier of the 3rd Dragoon Guards kisses a child before leaving to fight in Egypt, 1914.

The Grenadier Guards are watched by a crowd as they leave Wellington Barracks, London, for active service in France at the start of the First World War.

King George V takes the salute as the first Guards pass Buckingham Palace on their way to war in France.

A carrying party of British troops taking a batch of duckboards across the marshy ground of foreign fields during the First World War.

British troops occupying a section of trench in a ruined landscape.

British troops in France going 'up the line' to their trenches.

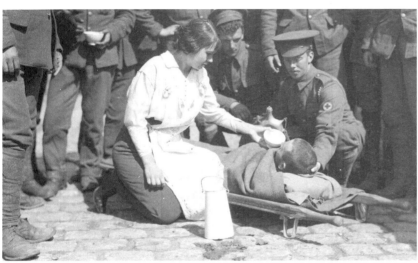

Red Cross work with British wounded in France during the First World War.

Women ticket collectors checking the ticket of a British soldier at Victoria Station, London, September 1914.

A First World War recruiting poster in London celebrates Michael O'Leary VC.

A soldier of the Royal Engineers wearing an early type of gas mask, c. 1915.

Facing page top: German soldiers lie dead in a belt of barbed wire in no man's land, 1915.

Facing page bottom: Carrying their Maxim machine-guns on their backs, German soldiers leave the trenches on the Eastern Front, 1915.

Right: Anti-German demonstrations along Crisp Street, Poplar, London in May 1915.

On Christmas Day hostilities ceased in favour of football. Here, officers and men of the 26th Divisional Train, ASC, enjoy a game at Salonika during the First World War, December 1915.

Canadian troops take their midday meal amid the mud caused by storms.

British 'tommies' of various English and Scottish regiments drawn up on a cobbled street in France, 1916.

Soldiers of the British Cavalry manning a Hotchkiss gun by a wood occupied by enemy infantry, 1916.

A British artilleryman pulls the lanyard to fire an eight-inch Howitzer, in France.

In a First World War trench, British troops sort through the belongings of German prisoners.

Right: British troops as they prepare to go over the top at the Battle of the Somme.

Facing page top: The face of a British soldier gazes out from a dug-out as a German soldier's body lies nearby at the Somme, July 1916.

Facing page bottom: A British soldier keeps watch on no man's land as his comrades sleep in a captured German trench near Albert, during the Battle of the Somme.

The Imperial War Cabinet pose for the camera, London, 1917.

Women engine cleaners on the South Western, during the First World War.

British troops with mules and a wagon pause in front of the ruins of the medieval cloth hall in Ypres, Belgium, at the end of the First World War, 1918.

The ruins of the *hôtel de ville* in Arras, northern France, damaged during the First World War.

King George V and Queen Mary on a visit to a Canadian hospital, 1918.

Servicemen and civilians celebrate together outside Buckingham Palace, November 1918, after the announcement of the armistice which ended the First World War. The royal family can be seen on the balcony of the palace.

A derelict British tank beside the infamous Menin Road near Ypres, Belgium, after the First World War.

The Queen inspects a rank of the WAAC at Aldershot, 1918.

Queen Mary in 1918 on board HMS *Queen Elizabeth*.

Field Marshal Sir Douglas Haig (left) outside Guildhall, London, in July 1919.

Road workers in Regent Street baring their heads in a tribute to the dead on Armistice Day, November 1919, a year after the end of the First World War.

A Royal Defence Force sentry at Somerset House, London, during the strike crisis of 1921.

A crowded platform at London's Paddington Station, during the 1924 rail strike.

Facing page top: Broadcasting the news during the General Strike of 1926, at a government centre for the maintenance of essential services.

Facing page bottom: A London bus, windows barricaded and driver screened by wire, during the General Strike.

A food convoy with military escort, passing through the docks on its way to Hyde Park, London, at the height of the General Strike.

May 1926: traffic returns to normal across Westminster Bridge, London, after the General Strike.

Hungry and angry, the Jarrow marchers – unemployed shipyard workers from north-east England – make their way to London, October 1936.

The Lancashire contingent of the 1932 Hunger Marchers passing through Gerrards Cross. Groups converged on London from all parts of the country.

Oswald Mosley, leader of the British Union of Fascists, addresses a supporters' meeting in the East End of London, October 1936.

A mounted policeman falls with his horse while following the Great Fascist March through south-east London, 1937.

A policeman charges into demonstrators with his truncheon during the 1937 Great Fascist March in London.

Neville Chamberlain, expecting 'peace in our time', returns from Munich after having talks with Adolf Hitler, 1939.

Facing page top: Sandbags in London's streets shortly after the outbreak of war, September 1939.

Facing page bottom: Workers fill shop fronts with sandbags in the streets of London during the Second World War.

London schoolboys, with gas masks and luggage, ready for evacuation to the safer countryside in September 1939.

London evacuees converging on Charing Cross for trains into the country.

War evacuees board a train for the west country, as their families remain in London to prepare for the worst.

Polish refugees in London during the Second World War.

Above left: Beneath a poster for National Service in Trafalgar Square, soldiers demonstrate a Vickers machine-gun and a range-finder to onlookers, as part of a big recruiting drive at the beginning of the Second World War.

As a measure to minimalise possible bomb damage, glass on the roof of London's Waterloo Station is replaced by asbestos sheets.

Left: A steel-hatted policeman on duty at the Bank traffic intersection, London, during the Second World War.

Sir Winston Churchill pictured
c. 1940.

A typical RAF fighter pilot in flying equipment in the early 1940s.

Whitley bombers flying in formation, 1941.

Facing page top: Soldiers of the Army Fire Service in action.

Facing page bottom: Disrupted service! A bus lies in a bomb crater after a German air raid during the Blitz in Balham, south London, 1940.

Close-up of the bus in a crater in Balham, London, following a bomb blast.

A huge crater caused by an enemy bomb in the Strand, London, during the Second World War.

Bomb damage caused by German aircraft at a coastal town in southern England: a crater now gapes by the side of an Anderson shelter, the occupants of which were unharmed.

A destroyed building burns in war-torn London following a German bombing raid.

Above: Tea-time in a field in Essex, where land-girls have brought acres under cultivation, 1941.

Boys from Battersea in London help to harvest fields on a farm in Buckinghamshire during the Second World War.

Facing page top: Bomb damage in central London after a recent air raid.

Facing page bottom: Children wearing gas masks at a Clerkenwell school, north London, during the Second World War.

A picture taken from the Press Association building on the night of 10 May 1941, as London was blitzed by German bombers.

Facing page: A corner of the small map room in the War Cabinet rooms, London. From this room a direct line ran to the Home Guard's advance headquarters. Wartime mementoes can be seen on the table – weekly analysis of flying-bomb raids and personal details of the *Luftwaffe* personnel brought down over Britain.

The after guns of HMS *Hood* pointing forward to get on the target. The vessel was sunk on 27 May 1941 while in action against the German pocket battleship *Bismarck*.

Women help in the construction of Britain's giant bomber, the Stirling, in 1942.

British soldiers are put through training exercises at a weapons training school during the Second World War. The toughening exercises included swimming with a full pack, climbing miniature mountains and being fired at.

A British Army Bren gun carrier about to pass the corpse of a German Afrika Korps soldier lying by the road in the wake of the decisive battle of El Alamein, October 1942.

Below right: The new Armstrong Whitworth flying-wing takes to the skies in 1943.

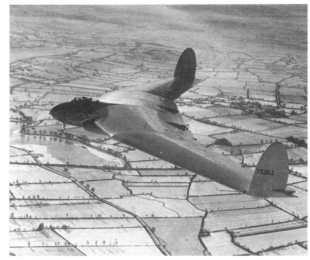

A pilot marks up the credit of a Hawker Typhoon plane during the Second World War. After several months of operations against the *Luftwaffe*, the Typhoon proved to be one of the most formidable aircraft in Fighter Command.

RAF pilots relaxing beside a Spitfire with their mascots.

Troops of the Canadian Army pose while undergoing a training session for realistic manoeuvres during the early 1940s.

The King and Queen, accompanied by Ernest Bevin, inspect a Ministry of Labour training centre in the home counties.

Facing page top: A British Army Sherman tank rumbles down the street past a policeman on its way to a south-coast port prior to the Normandy landings of June 1944. The censor has obliterated a sign in the background.

Facing page bottom: St Paul's Cathedral, London. Work begins on repairing the damage caused by *Luftwaffe* bombing raids on the City of London.

Sir Winston Churchill with his wife Clementine in 1945. Churchill is giving his famous victory sign.

Australian artillerymen bringing equipment ashore from a landing craft in readiness to support the advancing infantry with their famous 25-pounders, during the Second World War.

During their tour of the East End of London in May 1945, the King and Queen stop at Vallence Road, Stepney, which was badly damaged during a German rocket attack.

Below left: Queen Elizabeth is joined by members of the WVS, gathered round a vat of soup being prepared for delivery, during the war years.

Headlines from a week's newspapers (29 April – 5 May 1945) chronicling one of the momentous periods of the Second World War.

London, 8 May 1945: thousands of people gather in Trafalgar Square to mark VE-Day, celebrating the Allied victory over Germany and the end of the war in Europe.

VE-Day celebrations continue in London's East End.

Bodies discovered lying in a mass grave at Belsen concentration camp, Germany, after the Second World War.

The atomic bomb, 'Little Boy', which was dropped on Hiroshima on 6 August 1945.

Prime minister Clement Attlee (far right), Winston Churchill and other members of the Cabinet observing the two minutes' silence at the Cenotaph in Whitehall, London, on Remembrance Day, 1946.

Field Marshal Viscount Montgomery has a word for the BBC after his arrival home in April 1948 from Berlin. He had been in the German capital for talks with Soviet military governor Marshal Sokolovsky, regarding the tension which existed between the Allied forces there.

War Secretary 'Manny' Shinwell, later Lord Shinwell, sees off 1,500 officers and men of the 2nd Guards Brigade from Ocean Dock, Southampton, on their way to Malaya in the *Empire Trooper*, September 1948.

A female picket in London protesting with sandwich boards, demanding equal pay for women, October 1952.

Picture of London's Trafalgar Square, November 1956, during the National Council of Labour protest rally against the government's handling of the Suez situation.

Facing page top: RAF pilots take up position on the wing for a photo-call during active service with the United Nations in Korea, 1953.

Facing page bottom: A striker throws himself to the ground in front of a lorry at the Austin car works at Longbridge, Birmingham, in an attempt to stop the vehicle entering the factory. The strike was called in July 1956 by trade unions reacting to the dismissal of 6,000 workers.

British paratroops sit on a captured Russian tank at Port Said, at the northern end of the Suez canal, November 1956.

Royal Marine commandos greet their families after arriving at Plymouth from Port Said, December 1956.

Marchers carrying the nuclear disarmament symbol leave the Atomic Weapons Research Establishment at Aldermaston, Berkshire, March 1959, on a rally.

CND adherents begin another protest march from the Atomic Weapons Research Establishment at Aldermaston to Trafalgar Square, London, in April 1960. At the front is J.B. Priestley (wide-brimmed hat).

Anti-apartheid movement protesters marching in London from Hyde Park to Trafalgar Square, November 1963. Labour MP Barbara Castle is carrying a wreath to be placed at South Africa House.

The Rolling Stones, pictured in September 1964. Left to right: Bill Wyman, Keith Richards, Brian Jones, Mick Jagger and Charlie Watts.

Below left: Rolling Stones fans, their allegiance boldly proclaimed, gather at the Law Courts in London prior to the hearing of the appeals by Mick Jagger and Keith Richards against conviction and sentence on drug charges, 1967.

Rolling Stones guitarist Brian Jones going to the Law Courts to appeal against the nine-month sentence imposed after he was found guilty on drugs charges.

Marchers on London's Victoria Embankment after the start of the great anti-Vietnam War march, October 1968.

Below right: Tariq Ali (centre), one of the leaders, links arms with banner-carrying demonstrators at the head of the 1968 anti-Vietnam War march.

Derisory Nazi salutes from marchers as they pass the *Daily Express* building in Fleet Street during the demonstration march against war in Vietnam.

The mêlée as metropolitan policemen help an injured colleague in Grosvenor Square after several thousand anti-Vietnam War demonstrators attempted to break through the strong cordon at the approaches to the American embassy in London.

People move to and from the Bogside area of Londonderry after a night of rioting in which at least five people were shot dead, August 1969.

Women pushing a pram along Crumlin Road, Belfast, make a detour around the legs of a soldier lying with his Bren gun trained on Hooker Street – one of the trouble spots in riots which flared during August 1969.

Confrontation in Belfast, September 1969: tense moments as steel-helmeted troops, with their rifles pointing skywards, are confronted by angry residents.

Troops approach anti-internment marchers who demonstrated near Magilligan internment camp in defiance of a ban on marches by the Stormont authorities, January 1972.

Ulster Special Constabulary members parade through Belfast, April 1972.

Barrister James Crespi, wounded and bandaged, being helped away after the Old Bailey bomb explosion in London, March 1973.

Flames leap amid the smoke pouring from the House of Commons, June 1974, after a bomb blast in the crypt chapel.

The outside of the Mulberry Bush public house and surrounding buildings in central Birmingham, the day after the devastating IRA bomb of 21 November 1974.

The Balcombe Street siege, December 1975, when a gang of four highly trained IRA men was cornered by police and held a middle-aged couple hostage in their central London home. The terrorists gave themselves up after a six-day stand-off when the SAS were called in.

Police struggle to hold back hundreds of pickets as a workers' bus approaches the Grunwick film processing plant in Willesden, north London, October 1977, during the industrial dispute there.

The mangled remains of the car belonging to Airey Neave, Conservative spokesman for Northern Ireland. A bomb explosion had ripped it apart, killing Mr Neave as he drove out of the underground car park at the Houses of Parliament, March 1979.

Security forces on the balcony at the Iranian Embassy in London, just before two explosions and a forced entry ended the six-day siege at the building in May 1980.

BBC sound recordist Sim Harris – one of the British hostages – scrambles to safety while flames billow from the window at the Iranian Embassy, London, as the siege is ended.

Black and blue: a local youth confronts a senior police officer in Brixton, south London, during the period of rioting in April 1981.

Top left: A police officer being helped away by colleagues in Brixton, south London, when 23 police officers were injured in renewed fighting with black and some white youths, April 1981.

Middle left: Three masked men fire rifle shots over the coffin of republican hunger striker Bobby Sands at a pause in the funeral procession to the Milltown cemetery, Belfast, in May 1981.

Bobby Sands' weeping mother Rosaleen, supported by her husband and daughter, at the graveside of the IRA man during his funeral in Belfast, May 1981.

The union flag and white ensign being raised on South Georgia after the island's recapture by the British, May 1982. South Georgia is 800 miles east of the Falklands.

Royal Marine John Henderson mans a machine-gun above the flight-deck of HMS *Hermes* as dawn breaks over the South Atlantic during the Falklands conflict.

Survivors of HMS *Sir Galahad* are hauled ashore by colleagues at Bluff Cove, East Falkland, after an Argentinian air attack in June 1982 during the Falklands War. The ship (smoking in the background) was eventually towed out to sea and sunk as a war grave.

HMS *Antelope* explodes in San Carlos Bay, off East Falkland. A member of the frigate's crew was killed attempting to diffuse an Argentinian bomb, lodged in the ship's engine room, when it blew up.

Dead horses covered up alongside wrecked cars at the scene of carnage in Rotten Row, Hyde Park, after an IRA bomb exploded as the Household Cavalry were passing. The bomb – the first of two in London on the same day, 20 July 1982 – killed four soldiers and seven of their horses.

Police and firemen at the still-smouldering bandstand in Regent's Park, London, following the IRA bomb blast which killed six people and left others seriously injured. The bomb, the second in London on 20 July 1982, exploded during a performance by the Royal Green Jackets' band.

A sit-down protest from the women peace campaigners trying to blockade the Greenham Common airbase in Berkshire, December 1982. Police started to remove them from the gates of the base, which had been chosen as a Cruise missile site.

Below right: Former Labour Party leader Michael Foot (centre) leading a CND demonstration in London, 1983.

Facing page top: Fighting breaks out on the picket line at Tilmanstone Colliery, Kent, as miners returning to work face the fury of their colleagues (whose strike was solid until September 1984).

Facing page bottom: Arthur Scargill, president of the NUM, addressing a rally in Barnsley, September 1984.

A picket wearing a toy police helmet faces police at a mine near Selby, where violence flared during the lengthy miners' strike.

Tory chairman John Selwyn Gummer outside the Grand Hotel, Brighton, after an IRA bomb blast which claimed five lives and injured many other people during the week of the Conservatives' 1984 party conference.

A building is completely ablaze and a car overturned on a street corner of Brixton, south London, during disturbances in September 1985.

News International's picturesque new print plant at Wapping, east London, photographed in January 1986.

Top right: A notice explaining security measures at the entrance of the News International print plant at Wapping, 1986.

Middle right: News International proprietor Rupert Murdoch holds copies of his *Sun* and *Times* papers, produced at his new high-technology print works.

Marchers descend on Wapping in February 1982 to picket the print plant in support of print union SOGAT '82, who were in dispute with Rupert Murdoch's News International.

Faces of fury across the age barrier outside Rupert Murdoch's Wapping print works, March 1986, as the dispute rages on.

Deputy Assistant Commissioner Wyn Jones displays to the press some of the missiles thrown at police during picket-line violence outside the News International plant at Wapping.

March 1988: an injured man is aided by mourners (including Sinn Fein vice-president Martin McGuinness, left) at Milltown cemetery, Belfast, after a gun and bomb attack there. Three people were killed during the incident, which disrupted the funerals of three IRA members shot dead in Gibraltar.

Protesting prisoners at Risley Remand Centre, Cheshire, line up on the roof before ending their three-day occupation of D Wing, May 1989.

Great War veterans, Maurice Greenwood, 95 (left) and Joe Armstrong, 94, pictured in France for the Remembrance service at the Lochnagar Crater. The crater had been caused by the explosion which began the Battle of the Somme in 1916. The service was part of a special fund-raising weekend in July 1989 to commemorate that battle's anniversary.

Gerard Conlon, one of the Guildford Four, outside the Old Bailey saluting freedom on his release after the Court of Appeal quashed his sentence, October 1989.

A policeman grapples with a man in Lower Regent Street during the riots that broke out in central London at the end of the anti-poll tax demonstration, March 1990.

Veteran war correspondent Richard McMillan at Buckingham Palace in March 1990, about to hand in his treasured OBE in protest against the government's introduction of the community charge (poll tax), which he called 'abominable'.

Crowds choke Whitehall during an anti-poll tax
demonstration in London, March 1990.

Labour MP Tony Benn addresses a mass of protesters
against the poll tax, Trafalgar Square, London, March
1990.

Police Commander Bernard Lockhurst with some of the missiles used during the anti-poll tax riots in central London, in which more than 40 people were injured and thousands of pounds' worth of damage was caused.

Green Party spokesman and TV presenter David Icke, with his wife Linda, on the Isle of Wight, holding his summons before appearing at the magistrate's court for alleged non-payment of the poll tax.

Facing page top: A crazed protester kicks the window of a fast food store during the rioting in central London, March 1990.

Facing page bottom: Police survey the wreckage caused after anti-poll tax protesters ran riot on the streets of central London.

Two anti-poll tax protesters during demonstrations in Kennington Park, south London, October 1990.

Protesters from the Animal Liberation Front, following their raid on a laboratory owned by Boots the Chemist, London, November 1990.

One of the six RAF Tornado GR1 planes from 14
Squadron, Bruggen, Germany, *en route* for duty in the
Gulf War, January 1991.

'B' Company of the Royal Scots receive their injections
against chemical attack in the Gulf, February 1991.

Facing page: Grim aftermath of the Gulf War as the oilfields of Kuwait continue to burn, March 1991.

British soldiers from the Royal Pioneer Corps celebrate as they listen to news of Allied air strikes, from their front line dug-outs in the Saudi Arabian desert during the 1991 Gulf War.

Crowds march from the Embankment, central London, in protest against the Gulf War, January 1991.

A contemplative onlooker during an anti-Gulf War rally in Trafalgar Square, January 1991.

Flight-lieutenant John Peters, captured and interrogated by the Iraqis during the Gulf War, gives a reading at the Remembrance service in Glasgow, May 1991.

The Birmingham Six celebrate outside the Old Bailey in London, March 1991, after their convictions were quashed. Left to right: John Walker, Paddy Hill, Hugh Callaghan, Chris Mullen MP (who had campaigned for the men's release), Richard McIlkenny, Gerry Hunter and William Power.

Police in riot gear hold back demonstrations during an anti-racist march in London, October 1993.

Sinn Fein President Gerry Adams (right) raised eyebrows when he carried the coffin of Thomas Begley at the IRA man's funeral in Belfast, October 1993.

In January 1996 protesters against the controversial Newbury Bypass climb trees to save them from the chainsaw, while security guards below link arms to keep further saboteurs away.

Armed prisoners prepare for the second night of siege in January 1996 at Strangeways Prison, Manchester.

A building damaged by the blast when a bomb went off in the vicinity of London's Canary Wharf, February 1996.

RUC officers under petrol bomb attack on the Ormeau Road, Belfast, after trouble flared when an Apprentice Boys' march was prevented from walking through a Catholic area of the city, April 1996.

The sickening scene of total devastation in Manchester city centre caused by a massive IRA bomb explosion, June 1996.

RUC officers stand guard in case of trouble from the 10,000 Orangemen parading at Drumcree parish church, Portadown, 1996.

Basil and Josephine Cook, from Norfolk, catch up with the latest news before the start of July 1997's Countryside Protest Rally against anti-hunting laws, Hyde Park, London.

Loyalists confront riot police during the stand-off at Drumcree, Portadown in July 1998.

Firemen and RUC officers inspect the damage caused by a huge terrorist bomb explosion in Omagh, August 1998.

Crew of HMS *Invincible* keep fighting fit as they exercise on the hangar deck. Their ship was joining NATO forces off the Balkan coast to boost Britain's contribution to airstrikes against Serbian military targets during the Kosovo conflict, 1999.